MAIDSTONE CORPORATION TRANSPORT

1904–1974

ERIC BALDOCK

AMBERLEY

I am grateful to all the people who have taken pictures of Maidstone Corporation trams and buses over the years. Many of the earliest views are from commercial postcards, especially by the local firms of Young & Cooper and G. A. Cooper. The use of many original postcards from my own collection, and that of Irene Hales, ensures crisp reproduction. Another important source is from official photographs commissioned by vehicle manufacturers or by Maidstone Corporation itself.

The first enthusiast pictures came in the late 1920s, from early tram enthusiasts such as Dr H. A. Whitcombe, who visited Maidstone in around 1929. An early bus enthusiast and member of the Omnibus Society, John Parke visited Maidstone with his camera around 1935. My thanks go to Alan Oxley, Photographic Archivist of the Omnibus Society, for sorting out his pictures for me and some other Maidstone pictures from the OS collection.

Another of the pioneering bus photographers was Lewisham-based W. J. Haynes. He was a regular visitor to Maidstone from the 1930s for over 30 years. He worked for London Transport and had access to film during the Second World War. He kindly made his pictures available to the M&D and East Kent Bus Club for previous publications. On his death much of his vast negative collection passed to the Southdown Enthusiasts Club and I am grateful for their permission to use his work in this book. Particular thanks go to Calvin Churchill, SEC Photographic Officer, for looking through the negatives and printing some that I had not obtained in the past.

The work of other photographers has, over the years, joined my personal collection or that of the M&D and East Kent Bus Club (www.mdekbusclub.org). In some cases the original photographer has now died, but they had previously given their permission to use their photographs or donated their pictures to the club. Brian Weeden, MDEKBC Photographic Officer, has also been a great help in supplying prints for this book. Known contributors include Mick Comfort, Richard Ratcliffe, Lyndon Rowe and the late Frank Wright.

Richard Lewis, John Aldridge, Richard Rosa and the late Arnold Richardson have all supplied prints from their collections; the latter was the source of the early coloured trolleybus views, but the name of the original photographer is not known.

More colour views have come from the cameras of Mike Hodges, Paul Hollingsbee, Ian Paterson and Barry Ovenden, while my own efforts start in 1970.

I have recorded the original source of all the pictures where known, but some of the views have no details of the photographer or just a name, with no contact details. If anyone can show that they hold the copyright for any views used here, I will gladly supply a complimentary copy.

The late Len Leaver rescued a number of items from the rubbish bins at the depot for me in about 1976, and his daughter, Karen, has subsequently donated further items.

Finally, thanks to Paul Hollingsbee and Nicholas King for checking the text and to all the previous works listed in the bibliography – especially the publications of the M&D and East Kent Bus Club – that have been consulted, as well as source documents including the *Kent Messenger* and Maidstone Council minutes.

First published 2012

Amberley Publishing
The Hill, Stroud
Gloucestershire, GL5 4EP

www.amberley-books.com

British Library Cataloguing in Publication Data.
A catalogue record for this book is available from the British Library.

ISBN 978 1 4456 0820 4

Typeset in 10pt on 12pt Sabon.
Typesetting and Origination by Amberley Publishing.
Printed in the UK.

Contents

Introduction and General History

Maidstone is the administrative centre of Kent and is situated on the River Medway. The town's development was closely linked to trade on the river and industries related to the local agriculture. Brewing, food manufacture, agricultural machinery, papermaking and vehicle manufacturing were key industries.

Maidstone Corporation began operation of a single tramline from the High Street to Barming (Fountain Inn) on 14 July 1904, joined by further lines to Loose (King's Arms) from 16 October 1907 and Tovil (Rose Inn) from 9 January 1908.

The Loose route initially ran to the Queen's Monument, but was cut back to the Cannon from 26 November 1907. For the summer of 1909 it was extended to run to the 'South Eastern' station (Maidstone West). This was largely at the behest of Councillor Edmund Vaughan (who was chairman of the transport committee from 1904 to 1913), whose builder's merchant business was coincidentally near the station at 4 Tonbridge Road. It was found that reversing trams here impeded the Barming route and this was quickly discontinued. The Tovil route initially ran to the Queen's Monument, but by 1910 this also terminated at the Cannon. This was to be the maximum extent of the tram system, some 5.25 route miles.

The main depot was located on the Tonbridge Road, just short of the Barming terminus, near the junction with Queens Road, and the Loose route was partially worked from a four-car outstation at Pickering Street.

Despite many years of discussions and abortive plans, the remaining areas of the town were not covered by the corporation's services until the bus operation began from 7 April 1924. The first route ran between London Road (Queen's Avenue) and Penenden Heath. Another new route from 14 May 1926 linked Park Avenue (St Luke's Church) and Hackney Road. Initial buses were Maidstone-built Tilling-Stevens petrol-electric single-deckers.

Double-deck trolleybuses replaced the Barming trams from 1 May 1928. Further omnibus routes ran to Sutton Road (Mangravet Avenue) from 20 July 1928 and replaced the Tovil trams from 1 August 1929. A second batch of trolleybuses allowed the last trams – to Loose – to be replaced from 12 February 1930, with a through route from Barming to Loose and a new spur along the Sutton Road as far as Grove Road, which gave 5 route miles of trolleybus operation. This then allowed the Mangravet Avenue buses to be diverted to Foster Clark Estate from the same date. From 19 January 1931 this was reduced to peak hour only operation and extended to Plains Avenue.

On 28 February 1931 an infrequent service was introduced between Queens Road (Malling Terrace) and St Paul's Church. A further new route commenced on 15 January 1934, linking Holland Road and Mote Park Estate. Cross-town links were revised from 1 April 1939, so that Tovil was connected to Holland Road and Park Avenue and Hackney Road with Mote Park Estate.

A single batch of Leyland Lions appeared in 1929, followed by more Tilling-Stevens, by now with conventional transmission. A major change in policy from 1934 saw

Crossley double-deckers join the fleet, to replace the oldest single-deckers. During the war, nine Guy Arab buses and five Sunbeam trolleybuses were supplied, with bodywork to the usual utility standard.

The Second World War placed strains on operations, with mileage operated falling slightly but the number of passengers carried increasing considerably. The worst incident to disrupt operations was the bombing of Mill Street on 31 October 1940, which severed the trolleybus route. As a result, emergency arrangements (including temporary wiring) were made for two-way working via Lower Stone Street and Gabriel's Hill. General Manager Mr Lambert's tenure in office was extended past his due retirement date; he was finally released in 1946 after 35 years at the helm.

The Loose depot closed with the tramway in 1930, but the Tonbridge Road depot was extended several times over the years. Space was always tight, resulting in trolleybuses having to reverse into the Tonbridge Road. There were some abortive plans to provide improved depot facilities, including the purchase of land off the Loose Road, near the Wheatsheaf Inn, in 1924, which was sold again in 1930 after being used to scrap some of the trams. A further scheme saw land at Cripple Street purchased in 1946 and sold again in 1954.

The first post-war bus route expansion served the new housing estate of Ringlestone from 15 July 1946 and the trolleybus network was extended to Barming Bull Inn on 22 May 1947.

On 15 September 1947 the Tovil to Park Avenue and Holland Road service was modified by the removal of the tortuous portion of the route through Wyke Manor Road, Union Street and Wheeler Street. It was instead routed via King Street and Sittingbourne Road to Holland Road and thence Park Avenue.

The vast Shepway Estate, to the south-east of the town centre, was first served with a route to Kent Avenue via Plains Avenue from 5 January 1948. Operationally, the Ringlestone service was initially linked to London Road, but from 9 February 1948 it was diverted to run to Cherry Orchard Estate (just off the Tonbridge Road, near the depot) via Queens Road. Then, from 10 January 1949, Ringlestone was linked to the Mote Park Estate service and then extended in stages to Derby Road from 24 March 1952 and to Oxford Road from 26 April 1952.

Reverting to 1948, from 19 April, the Penenden Heath terminus was moved to Peel Street Hedges. The London Road end of this route was extended to Allington Way from 6 March 1950.

A further route into Shepway commenced from 26 March 1956, running via Plains Avenue to Westmorland Road. From 22 October 1956, the Park Avenue route was extended to Hatherall Road. Buses first served Palace Wood, off the London Road, from 21 December 1959.

Two batches of Daimlers joined the bus fleet in 1947 and 1949, with twenty-six Leyland Titans, in seven batches, joining the fleet from 1956 to 1963.

A batch of twelve Sunbeam trolleybuses replaced the pre-war fleet in 1946/7, and later second-hand vehicles came from Llanelli (two), Brighton (two) and Hastings (five), while the five utility trolleybuses were re-bodied in 1960.

The trolleybus network was further extended along the Sutton Road to Nottingham Avenue (21 June 1954), then into Park Wood - Brishing Lane (4 May 1959) and Park Wood shops from 18 July 1963. The latter extensions were built using largely second-hand equipment from Brighton. The days of the system were numbered, due to the higher cost of vehicles and the inflexibility of operation. A full council meeting on

29 April 1964 ratified a transport committee report to end trolleybus operation within four years, a target that was actually achieved in three years. The final change to the system took place from 13 December 1964, with the opening of Bishop's Way – a new road linking Mill Street with the High Street end of Maidstone Bridge. The northern end of Mill Street became one-way and services were diverted along the new road; this left the main town pick-up stop for Barming at a rather bleak location by the river, instead of by the Cannon. This diversion also affected inward motor-bus services from the south of town.

Eight Leyland Atlanteans were delivered in 1965 to begin trolleybus replacement and a second batch of eight resulted in the end of trolleybus operation on 15 April 1967. Four more in 1968 resulted in the withdrawal of the last Daimlers, while the final deliveries of two more batches of four allowed the first Titans to be stood down.

Depot capacity remained an issue, especially during times of transition within the fleet. As a result, the former Loose tram shed was hired from 1959 to 1967 for the storage of non-operational vehicles. Various other sites were used in the period between 1965 and 1967 to facilitate the replacement of the trolleybuses.

In 1968 a large site was purchased in Armstrong Road and the new depot here replaced Tonbridge Road from 5 January 1969. This was an appropriate location as the name Armstrong Road commemorates Alderman T. Armstrong, who was chairman of the transport committee from 1925 to 1946.

Routes continued to be extended or introduced to serve the new housing being built around the town. From 11 October 1965 the service to Barming, Banky Meadow started, followed by Gatland Lane from 4 June 1968. From 19 June 1968, some Park Wood journeys were extended to Selby Road. With the opening of the new depot, from 5 January 1969 the Westmorland Road service was diverted via Postley Road and Armstrong Road, largely as a staff facility, but also providing a service to new and existing housing in the area. One strange working as a result of the depot move was the last inward journey from Hackney Road to the depot, which ran via Hartnup Street to reach the Tonbridge Road. From 14 July 1969 outward buses on the London Road service terminated by a loop working of Conway Road, Headingley Road and Allington Way; this resulted in the stop being moved within the turning circle so that it could be reached from Allington Way.

In order to save money, trials with 'pay as you enter' operation with Atlanteans took place in 1968 and a gradual conversion of operations began from 1969. Initially such workings were limited to evening and Sunday operation, but gradually spread to all-day operation on most routes. Titans took over the peak extras on the former trolleybus services, while Atlanteans began to appear on other routes. After the arrival of the final deliveries of Atlanteans, conductor operation was limited to the Ringlestone–Oxford Road trunk route, some infrequent services and peak hour extras.

A major town centre traffic scheme from 5 April 1970 resulted in many services being rerouted, with key features including the removal of traffic from much of Week Street. The flow in Pudding Lane was reversed and was now used by buses from Ringlestone and Penenden Heath, while the outward stops for these locations were banished to Fairmeadow. The main feature was the introduction of one-way traffic southbound in Upper Stone Street, and northbound in Sheal's Crescent, Hayle Road and College Road. At this stage Mote Road had not been widened, so there was no access from here into Knightrider Street. As a result, buses from Oxford Road initially had to run via Upper Stone Street, Campbell Road and College Road.

To avoid this peripatetic routing, from 10 August 1970, buses towards Ringlestone from Oxford Road were diverted via Barton Road to join the one-way system, while both directions on the Hackney Road–Oxford Road route were operated via King Street, Ashford Road and Square Hill Road.

The final service changes of the corporation era included routes to new housing at Senacre Wood – Woolley Road (7 September 1970), Vinters Park – Alkham Road (9 August 1971) and Park Wood – Highcroft Green (10 January 1972), which was served by extending some Westmorland Road buses across the Sutton Road into Park Wood. On 7 August 1972 Hackney Road ceased to be used as a terminus, and the Oxford Road route was extended to turn at Gatland Lane, while the infrequent service between Gatland Lane and the town centre was withdrawn; as was the single late night depot journey via Hartnup Street. The single remaining lunch-time trip via Cherry Orchard Estate ceased from 9 August 1971.

Some buses on the Loose route were finally extended to serve the village centre from 12 March 1973.

The Maidstone Corporation era came to an end on 31 March 1974 with the retirement of Walter Kershaw, the General Manager since 1953, and the transfer of operations to the new Maidstone Borough Council. The final years of Maidstone Corporation had been relatively quiet, but under the new organisation change was rapid and is recorded in my companion volume *Maidstone Borough Buses 1974–1992*.

Eric Baldock
Maidstone, February 2012

Trams 1904–1930

Maidstone Corporation Tramway opened on 14 July 1904, with a single route to the western suburb of Barming. The only known view of the opening ceremony is this postcard of the official first tram (presumably No. 1) with the civic party outside the town hall and three others behind at the Queen's Monument loaded with passengers keen to try out this new form of transport in the town. (*Author's collection*)

This postcard view of tram 3 at St Michael's Church on the Tonbridge Road was taken very soon after opening. It exists as both a coloured and black and white postcard and as a picture in the tram timetable booklet. The line was generally single-track, set in the middle of the road. (*Author's collection*)

Tram 5 was photographed in the narrow part of the High Street, by Middle Row. Here the track ran in the south side gutter, which meant trams going against the flow towards the Queen's Monument. (*MDEKBC collection*)

A more distant view of a tram at the same top shows the single-track arrangement. Note that the track was restored to the centre in the wider part of the road, by the Cannon. (*Author's collection*)

Passing loops were provided about every quarter of a mile. This early Young & Cooper postcard shows tram 2 edging out of the loop at the Queen's Road junction. (*Author's collection*)

A later postcard taken at the same location, but looking towards town, with tram 3 waiting to pass the tram from town. The traction poles at the entrance to the depot can just be discerned in the distance, by the approaching tram. The streetlight on the junction has changed from gas to electricity between the two views. (*Author's collection*)

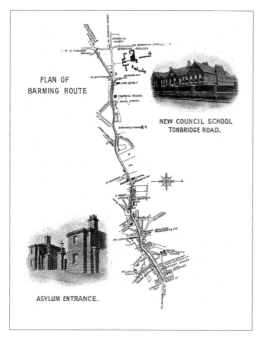

A map of the Barming route from the 1909 tram timetable. The maps in this timetable are the only known examples of any maps that were produced as part of the corporation's publicity. (*Author's collection*)

By the time this view was taken painted adverts were beginning to appear. Car No. 2 was posed outside St Andrew's School and the reservoir at Barming. (*MDEKBC collection*)

In this postcard view, taken at the Queen's Monument, even more adverts had appeared. The traction current supply box can be seen in the right foreground. (*Author's collection*)

A second postcard view of tram 2 shows the overhead arrangement here to avoid a traction pole in the middle of the road. Lefevre had by this time ceased to pay for the advert, which had been removed. (*Author's collection*)

The initial fleet consisted of just six trams, but such was the success of the service an extra vehicle was ordered for urgent delivery late in 1904 and No. 7 duly arrived in February 1905. This view shows it on the only double track section of the 1904 layout – over the Medway Bridge – with tram 5 waiting to go the other way. (*Irene Hales collection*)

A second route opened to Loose on 16 October 1907. This postcard of tram 12 is inscribed 'first tram's arrival at Loose terminus' and has attracted the attention of the local children. (*Irene Hales collection*)

Trams 1–7 were constructed by the Electric Railway & Tramway Carriage Works, Preston and sat twenty-six upstairs and twenty-two downstairs. They were 6 feet 6 inches wide and 27 feet 8 inches long. This builder's official photograph shows the completed tram 6, although the two lamps carried upstairs have either not been fitted or removed with the background. (*MDEKBC collection*)

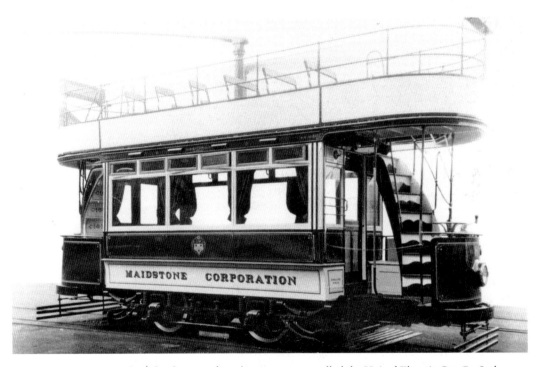

Trams 8–17 were built by the same firm, but it was now called the United Electric Car Co. Ltd. They were shorter (at 24 feet 8 inches), seating twenty-two upstairs and eighteen downstairs, but otherwise had only minor detail differences. They lacked the ornate scrollwork behind the stairs; also the headlamp was lower and a chain replaced the expanding gate that closed off the entrance at the driving-end. They were fitted with roller blind destination boxes from new, which also provided the lighting for the upper deck. (*MDEKBC collection*)

Postcard publishers were keen to record the new tram service. G. A. Cooper's picture shows tram 13 arriving at Loose from town and clearly shows the siding and passenger shelter. (*Author's collection*)

Young & Cooper recorded car 9 in this postcard looking in the other direction. Although the terminus was just beyond the town boundary, trams did not reach the centre of the village, which is down a steep hill beyond the tram. (*Author's collection*)

A close-up of tram 9 at the same location shows the circular traction current feeder box, which contained the circuit breakers. (*Author's collection*)

A map of the Loose route from the 1909 timetable. The vignette of tram 10 is the only known photo of a tram using the siding. The route was promoted for its 'lovely walks' and 'good places for refreshment in the village' – the siding was no doubt used for extra cars at busy times. (*Author's collection*)

The Loose route was double track along Mill Street, Knightrider Street and Upper Stone Street, but from Barton Road onwards it became single track, laid mostly on the east side of the road, with passing loops. This view, from an advert for the Swan Inn, shows the track on the east side of the road and Boughton Lane on the left. A four-car depot was provided at the junction of Pickering Street. (*Author's collection*)

Tram 17 at Loose in 1909 was photographed showing this short-lived 'S E Station' destination. It is thought that most of the single line sections were worked on a visual basis, as the passing loops were generally inter-visible. This was not the case between the crossing loop by the Loose depot and the terminus, and this was controlled by token working. In this postcard view, the tennis-racquet-shaped token can just be discerned in the conductor's hand. (*Author's collection*)

Meanwhile the third and final route, to Tovil, opened on 9 January 1908. It was a single-track from just beyond its junction with the Loose route by All Saints' Church, except for a single loop in the middle of King Edward Road and a double track section on the steep Tovil Hill. This view shows workers laying the track at the top of Tovil Hill. (*Irene Hales collection*)

Another Young & Cooper postcard, dating from about 1925, is looking down Tovil Hill towards the terminus at the Rose Inn, which can be seen behind the tram. Although there was some housing here, workers at the various paper mills were the main source of traffic. (*Author's collection*)

The crew stand by tram 11 at Tovil while the Young & Cooper photographer recorded this view before the Great War. The front dash was not used for advertising after the decision to fit the headlight on it, but the rest of the vehicle was well covered. (*Author's collection*)

A closer view, this time of car 12, shows the twin tracks up the hill and some of the paper mill buildings to the right. The stair risers were used exclusively for adverts for the local firm of Grant's (famous for its Morello Cherry Brandy) for almost the entire life of the trams. (*MDEKBC collection*)

The Tovil route ran initially to the Queen's Monument, as shown here by Tram 11, which was displaying Tovil on its blind. Behind it is the street watering car, and in the foreground the recently laid second track can be seen. The road is wet from the efforts of the watering car, but even so it had failed to deal with some of the horse dung – a major problem of this era. (*Author's collection*)

By 1910 the Tovil route was also revised to terminate at the Cannon, initially standing in the middle of the road, but later the layout was changed to include a siding in front of the Gas Company's shop at the end of Middle Row. (*Author's collection*)

The new track layout from 1907 featured a double track triangular junction (as shown in this postcard) between the High Street and new routes along Mill Street. The west side of Mill Street had to be demolished to allow the road to be widened before the line could be constructed. (*Author's collection*)

The other new junction was outside All Saints' Church and this postcard view, taken about 1920, of the church has nicely picked up the detail of both the track and the overhead. The Tovil route, to the left, became single track just after the main junction, allowing a tram towards Tovil to stand clear of the Loose route and wait for the inward tram from Tovil. (*Author's collection*)

In 1908, this un-numbered service tram was supplied by Mountain & Gibson Ltd of Bury. It was primarily a street-watering car, with a 300-gallon tank, but it was also fitted with revolving brooms and groove-scrapers, especially useful in the snow. These official views show it in the siding at the Barming terminus when new. It carried the ochre livery of the passenger trams, but with no white relief or lining-out. Street watering ended about 1921, as road surfaces improved and horse traffic was much reduced. (*MDEKBC collection*)

The final member of the tram fleet was one-person operated demi-car 18, purchased in 1909, to reduce operating costs on the Tovil route, where loadings were scant outside shift change times at the paper mills. This car sat nineteen passengers and ran regularly until 1919, when increased loadings resulted in the return of double-deck trams on the Tovil route. It was little used after that date and was dumped out the back of depot by 1926. This view is at the Barming terminus. (*Author's collection*)

From 1907 the track in the High Street was re-laid as double-track, but was still on the northerly side of the road, as the south-side was used by the various carrier's carts from the rural areas. Tram number 1 shows the modified headlamp position and the destination display that was added when the new routes were introduced. (*Author's collection*)

Another postcard view, this time taken from the end of the bridge in what must have been the summer of 1909, as car 12 is heading for Loose, having reversed at Maidstone West Station. (*Author's collection*)

This is the funeral of local brewer Ralph Fremlin on the 16 March 1910, with the rear end of the procession passing between the junctions of Barton Road and Sheal's Crescent. The Napier car in the foreground belonged to Ralph's brother, Richard, but it is the tram in the distance that is of interest. The adverts show it is car 11 again and a magnifying glass shows the destination as 'Cemetery' thus making this the only known photo of a special working. (*Author's collection*)

Moving on to 21 June 1922, with the unveiling of Maidstone's War Memorial outside the West station, and in the background two Barming trams are standing waiting for passengers to return after the event. The end of the double track section can be seen on the left and this is the point at which Loose trams had reversed in 1909. Behind the people standing on the roof of George Bunyard's shop, part of the name on the side of Edmund Vaughan's shop is visible. (*Author's collection*)

Above and below: Two postcard views of Maidstone Bridge from the Broadway, looking towards the High Street – the upper view, taken in about 1918, clearly shows the track and overhead. Over Christmas 1927 snow, followed by heavy rain, caused flooding which disrupted the operation of the trams. This view on 27 December shows what is almost certainly a Maidstone Corporation horse and cart carrying passengers through the floods. The bridge had been widened in 1927 and the overhead was also already in place for the forthcoming trolleybuses. (*Both Author's collection*)

During the First World War many men joined the services and women were employed to cover all conductor and some of the motorman positions. A lady motorman poses at the controls of number 6 in the depot yard. Her left hand is on the power controller and the right hand on the brake. (*MDEKBC collection*)

Another shot taken in the depot shows car 2 in its final condition, with the destination box lowered to above the driver's head and no lining-out around the fleetname. (*Dr H. A. Whitcombe/ Author's collection*)

The crew of number 7 and a fitter pose at the depot, with the presence of a lady conductor dating the view to during or soon after the war. (*MDEKBC collection*)

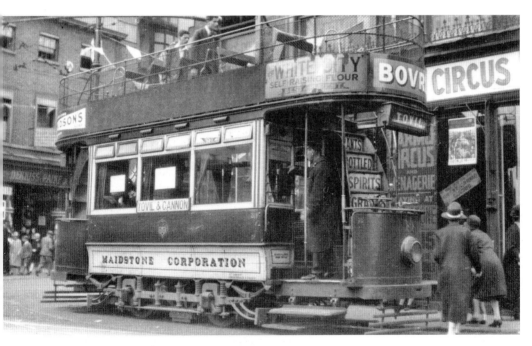

Towards the end of tram operation, Dr Whitcombe took a ride on tram 11 between the Cannon and Tovil and took several photographs. These photographs were produced as postcards, presumably for the growing enthusiast market rather than general sale. In the siding at the Cannon, the driver watches the conductor turn the boom. Care had to be taken to ensure the trams were the right way round, as the boom only rotated on one side and here the building was too close to make a turn on that side! (*Dr H. A. Whitcombe/Author's collection*)

This second view of tram 11 shows it at the Tovil terminus, with the paper mill behind. The crew were now happy to pose for the photographer. (*Dr H. A. Whitcombe/Author's collection*)

A final view of the tramway shows car 17 standing in the Wheatsheaf loop, at the junction between the Loose Road and Sutton Road. It was waiting to cross the outward tram running towards Loose and looks strangely out of place in the modern housing. The single-line track can be seen in the distance running on the east side of the road – it was fortunate that even at this late stage traffic was not heavy. (*Author's collection*)

Motor Buses 1924–1939

Maidstone Corporation had considered for some time how to serve parts of the town not covered by the trams and finally decided to run motor-buses on a route between Penenden Heath and London Road. The first buses were locally built by Tilling-Stevens. This official view was taken outside Preston Hall. (*MDEKBC collection*)

A view taken from a postcard of the Queen's Monument shows 2 (KK 9420) waiting to depart for Penenden Heath (from here it turned left into Week Street). The lack of any trolleybus overhead suggest it was taken in that year or 1927. The 'Tramways Dept.' had been dropped from the fleetname from January 1926, when the undertaking was renamed the Maidstone Corporation Transport Department. (*Author's collection*)

The initial bus fleet consisted of three of the normal control vehicles and two of larger half-cab type buses. This is 5 (KL 1651) at the Queen's Monument loading for the London Road– it now had 'Transport Dept' in the fleetname. There are two versions of this picture – the other one is without the young lady on the right. (*Courtesy Southdown Enthusiasts Club*)

Three more buses, with centre-entrance Beadle bodywork, came in 1926. This is 6 (KM 3937) in one of several known Tilling-Stevens official photographs of this vehicle outside Preston Hall. (*Author's collection*)

No. 8 (KM 3939) of the same batch loads for Hackney Road at the Queen's Monument stop. This is a later view with pneumatic tyres on the front axle. These were some of the last petrol-electrics built and the last for Maidstone. These vehicles were of similar concept to the modern hybrid, with the petrol engine generating electricity, which powered electric motors on the axle, but without battery power storage. (*Omnibus Society collection*)

This view shows one of a pair of Vickers-bodied Tilling-Stevens delivered in 1928 as 9/10 (KP 319/20). Like the trolleybuses delivered earlier in the same year, they had pneumatic tyres all round from new. (*MDEKBC collection*)

A change in purchasing policy resulted in the delivery of a batch of four Leyland Lions, with Ransomes, Sims & Jefferies bodywork, in 1929. The fleetname style was unique to this batch, which was numbered 19–22 and registered KP 8371 – 4. (*John Aldridge collection*)

In this view, 22 (KP 8374) was passing Maidstone East station on the Penenden Heath to London Road service. There are decorations visible in this view, including bunting on the roof of the bus, perhaps for the 1935 Silver Jubilee of King George V. (MDEKBC collection)

Beadle bodied Tilling-Stevens 30 (KJ 6881) of 1932 was also posed at Preston Hall when brand new and was still lacking its front registration plate. These were fitted with an AEC 7.7 litre engine and two similar vehicles followed early in 1933. (*MDEKBC collection*)

An early enthusiast's picture shows an unidentified Leyland Lion on the Mote Park Estate to Holland Road service about 1935. It was on the move turning by the Cannon from Mill Street to the High Street. As a result the bus is not sharp, but it can be seen that the fuel filler has been modified from the original design. (*John Parke/ Omnibus Society collection*)

As new housing was built along the London Road, the terminus moved to Little Buckland Lane in 1927 and had reached Grace Avenue by this unseasonable hailstorm of 19 June 1933. What seems to be one of the new Tilling-Stevens was turning at the terminus. (*Irene Hales collection*)

This view shows Tilling-Stevens 31 (KJ 6882), the other of the 1932 pair, working an outward Tovil service in Mill Street. Behind can be seen Rootes new garage, which later expanded to replace the tannery building on the right. (*Omnibus Society collection*)

Increasing traffic in the 1930s resulted in the first double-deck motor-buses arriving in January 1934. These were a pair of Crossley Condors with Crossley bodywork, as shown by this view of 35 (AKO 391) in Sandling Road. They carried a livery akin to the 1930 trolleybuses. (*Richard Lewis collection*)

The summer of 1934 saw two more double-deckers join the fleet. These were Beadle-bodied Crossley Mancunians and 36 (BKK 899) was recorded at the Cannon stop on the Penenden Heath service. Only these two buses carried this livery style. (*John Parke/Omnibus Society collection*)

1936 saw the delivery of two Park Royal-bodied Crossley Mancunians. This pre-delivery shot at the Park Royal factory records 39 (CKO 71) with its fleetname still incomplete. (*MDEKBC collection*)

Later batches of Crossleys reverted to Crossley bodywork. A pre-war commercial postcard taken from the town hall roof picks up 41 (EKM 395), new in 1937. The flags are out, indicating an event like cricket week. In this view, the band above the lower deck windows appears to be darker than the other brown areas. (*Author's collection*)

This is 40 (EKM 394) of 1937 at the Queens Monument stop on the service to Park Avenue. It is still in its original livery, but the white on the nearside wing suggests an early post-war view and again the flags are out. (*W. J. Haynes via SEC*)

42 (FKL 901) was new in 1938 and, together with sister 43, represented the final pre-war additions to the fleet. Probably on the same day, but on the opposite side of the Queen's Monument, it was taken loading up for London Road. Both these vehicles also appear to have darker brown above the lower deck windows. (*W. J. Haynes, Author's collection*)

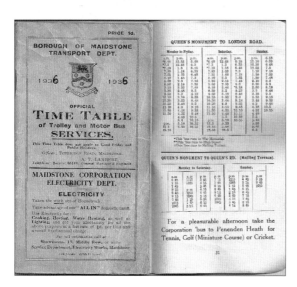

The pre-war style of timetable just listed departure times from key points. Sunday operation did not start until after the morning church services. A bus ticket and metal season ticket from this era are also shown. (*All author's collection*)

Trolleybuses 1928–1939

To replace the trams on the Barming route eight trolleybuses, numbered 11–18, came from Ramsomes, Sims & Jefferies of Ipswich. This is an RSJ official view before delivery and the fitting of its number plate. (MDEKBC collection)

The official views included interior shots – this is the upper deck looking forward – note the wooden roof. (*MDEKBC collection*)

On arrival at Maidstone the entire batch were posed on the Tonbridge Road, with 18 (KO 8896) leading. Despite the destination, they are lined up facing the town. The livery application was akin to that of the trams, with the brown front and rear mimicking the dash panels found on the trams (*MDEKBC collection*)

A slightly later view of the same vehicle – it has now gained a *Kent Messenger* advert – in almost the same part of the Tonbridge Road, but this time really heading for Barming. Operation in service began on 1 May 1928. (*Author's collection*)

A view inside the Tonbridge Road depot, with three of the new trolleybuses on the right and some trams on the left. Unlike the double-ended trams, which could be easily reversed in the depot, trolleybuses were always driven in and reversed out into the main road, a manoeuvre that became increasingly fraught as traffic increased. (*MDEKBC collection*)

For around two years ram tracks were retained between the depot and the town centre to service the remaining two routes, as shown by this postcard of the High Street. No. 11 (KO 8894) heads for Farming, while in the distance another member of the batch is at the Cannon stop and a Tilling-Stevens can also just be discerned. (*Author's collection*)

HIGH STREET, MAIDSTONE.

A later view of 17 (KO 8895) in much the same position, but with the tram tracks gone and a motor-bus just entering Mill Street on the civil service. (*Author's collection*)

Another rear view, this time of 16 (KO 8893) it is known that some registration numbers of this batch were swapped on overhaul, as 16 was new as KO 8894 – outside the shops on the corner of Queen's Road, just to the west of the depot. (*Author's collection*)

A close-up view of the passengers boarding 15 (KO 8892) at the Queen's Monument, with the town hall behind. No. 15 was originally KO 8893. (*Author's collection*)

Ransomes 13 (KO 8892) loads at the Queen's Monument for Barming, while the crew take a breather. Behind is Tilling-Stevens 4 (KL 1650) on the London Road service. (*John Aldridge collection*)

Above and below: Commercial postcard publishers were out in force to record the new trolleybuses, as views showing trams were suddenly dated. In two views from the same (unknown) publisher, the first shows number 12 (KO 8543) at the Queen's Monument and the other shows 18 (KO 8896) on the bridge, with Tilling-Stevens 5 (KL 1651). (*Both Irene Hales collection*)

Last of the batch, 18 (KO 8896) stands on the eastbound side of the Queen's Monument in original condition – the blind has already been set for the return to Barming (*Richard Lewis collection*)

Seven more trolleybuses joined the fleet, this time built by English Electric, to facilitate the replacement of the last trams on the Loose route from 12 February 1930. Here, in a posed view when new, 24 (KR 352) demonstrates its manoeuvrability. To the right, Mill Street is shut to remove the tram tracks. Note the white roof and all brown lower rear panel, not evident in later views of this batch. (*MBEKBC collection*)

A later view of 26 (KR 354) at the Barming terminus, showing its brown roof and white lower panel, twin rear number plates and its bamboo pole deployed to position its booms on the overhead. (*Author's collection*)

26 (KR 354) was photographed at the Barton Road stop in Upper Stone Street. The booms were on a single pivot (and to obtain reverse the booms had to be swapped over) and the wires were spaced 12 inches apart at this time. (*W. J. Haynes/ Author's collection*)

At the same stop, but at a different date – note the changes in the background – 23 (KR 351) was working a well-loaded Sutton Road journey. (*W. J. Haynes/ Author's collection*)

A new spur from the Wheatsheaf was opened from along the Sutton Road to Grove Road, with alternate trips from Barming running here and to Loose. Ransomes 13 (KO 8544) stands at the Grove Road turning circle (*W. J. Haynes/Author's collection*)

An interesting comparison between the two styles of trolleybuses at the Queen's Monument. A Ransomes example heads for Sutton Road, with an English Electric one behind on the Loose service. This is a rare photograph of one of the second batch in service with a white roof. (*Richard Rosa collection*)

After the replacement of the Loose trams by trolleybuses, the service ran out via Gabriel's Hill and Lower Stone Street, but returned via the old tram route along Knightrider Street and Mill Street. As a result the Cannon stop became the main town centre stop for Barming (provoking letters of complaint in the local press). No. 17 (KO 8895) was recorded here in a revised livery, with a brown roof and new style fleetname. (*W. J. Haynes via SEC*)

Commercial postcards showing the English Electric trolleybuses are less common, but 29 (KR 357) appeared in this view of the Granada cinema in Lower Stone Street, which opened in 1934, again in the later style livery. (*Author's collection*)

The final view in this section shows a Ransomes trolleybus at the Queen's Monument during the celebration of King George V's Jubilee in 1935. Note the decorations on the bank and its staff getting a superb view from their vantage point, while the crew are making full use of the opening windows on the top deck. (*MDEKBC collection/ Richard Ratcliffe*)

The War Years

This view of a service van shows the detailing in the livery. It was taken in Heath Road, Barming, and the mask on the headlamp dates this view to around 1940. It is probably Bedford GKL 317 when new. (*MDEKBC collection*)

Above and previous page below: With the outbreak of war in 1939, production of buses was frozen, as output was switched to war materials. By 1940 limited numbers of partially completed vehicles were released and Maidstone took delivery of four 'unfrozen' Crossleys. No. 45 (GKK 984) poses at the usual spot in Tonbridge Road, complete with masked headlights and white-edged wings and partial blackout on the windows. The exact livery is unclear – the waist-rail is darker than the lower panels – it may be two shades of brown or brown and black. (*John Aldridge collection/MDEKBC collection*)

Later in the war, production resumed with a limited range of chassis and angular, utility bodywork using mostly wood. Maidstone was initially allocated a pair of Duple-bodied Guy Arabs, delivered in 1942. Many utility buses were delivered in brown- or grey-based liveries, but here there were few concessions to the war – only the grey roof and no lining-out on the white. No. 49 (GKT 165) was photographed at the London Road (Grace Avenue) terminus when almost new. (*W. J. Haynes/ Richard Lewis collection*)

Maidstone was also allocated five Sunbeam Ws with Park Royal bodies, delivered in 1943 and 1944. No. 58 (GKP513) was posed on the Tonbridge Road when new in 1944. The band above the lower deck windows was probably black. (*MDEKBC collection*)

This view shows Ransomes 16 (KO 8894) at the Barming terminus, complete with a wartime advert – it retained its all brown lower rear. Note also the white paint on the traction pole to aid vision in the blackout. (*Author's collection*)

Maidstone Corporation received a total of nine Guy Arab motor-buses between 1942 and 1945. The first six were posed, almost certainly on Penenden Heath, in full wartime condition. Nearest the camera is Duple-bodied 49 (GKT 165) and next is Weymann-bodied 53 (GKN 156), which has anti-blast mesh on its side windows. (*MDEKBC collection*)

This view of Weymann-bodied 52 (GKN 155) was taken on the same occasion. Unusually, the front fleet number was carried on the front bulkhead rather than under the driver's window. Lining-out can be seen on the lower brown band. (*MDEKBC collection*)

A delivery view of the other one of the pair, 53 (GKN 156) shows detailed differences – the brown waistband is thinner (observe the bottom of the crest is just on the white) and not lined out, while the area of white on the front wing is also smaller. (*MDEKBC collection*)

Above and below: Bill Haynes visited Maidstone around the end of the war and recorded unfrozen Crossley 45 (GKK 984) and Park Royal-bodied Guy utility 59 (HKE 661) at the Penenden Heath terminus. Rather than masking the headlights, later wartime deliveries had very small headlights. The Guy also clearly shows the contrast between the brown guttering and grey roof. Unlike the first six Guy Arabs, the white was continued round the front offside corner, in pre-war fashion. (*W. J. Haynes/Author's collection and via SEC*)

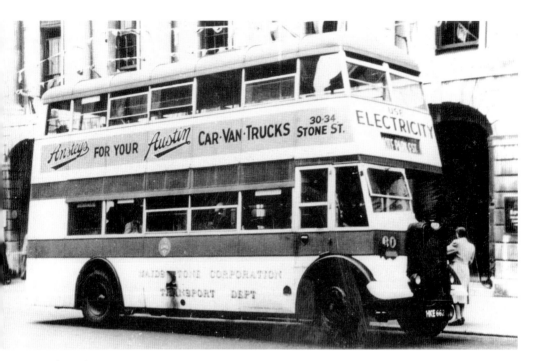

Another of the utility Guys, 60 (HKE 662), still in wartime livery, but with flags which suggest it is probably after the war, stands at the Queen's Monument on the Mote Park Estate service. (*MDEKBC collection*)

One of the 1940 batch of Crossleys, complete with masked headlights, waits at the Mote Park Estate terminus in Upper Road. The crew are taking a break away from the bus, while a handful of passengers have already taken their seats. (*Richard Lewis collection*)

Motor Buses 1946–1965

The first post-war buses were a batch of Northern Coachbuilders-bodied Daimler CVG6s delivered in 1947. They carried a new livery, also found on the 1946 batch of trolleybuses, with a lighter shade of brown and more white. At the same time the fleet name was reduced to just 'Maidstone Corporation'. No. 75 (JKO 639) was recorded in this official view in what looks like Mote Park. (*MDEKBC collection*)

A second batch of Daimlers was delivered in 1949, this time with bodywork by Brush and yet another revised livery, with much increased areas of brown. No doubt the high proportion of white in the previous application proved too difficult to keep clean in the days of coal fires and carbon deposit from the trolleybus overhead. (*MDEKBC collection*)

When new, three of the batch were hired to London Transport, working from Sutton Garage. This photograph shows 82 (LKJ 782) during its stay in London, with an LT roundel on the grille and depot code and running number behind the cab door. Note the absence of a fleet name, although the Maidstone crest was carried. (*Author's collection*)

An early view of Daimler 80 (LKJ 780) in service in Maidstone, in original livery and fleetname about 1950. (*B. J. Walters, Author's collection*)

The dullest fleet livery was that used in the early to mid-1950s, which was all over dark brown, relieved only by black wings and white lower deck window surrounds. No. 80 (LKJ 780) photographed just about to cross the Medway bridge from the Westborough side. (*R. Hannay/Author's collection*)

No. 77 (LKJ 777) was decorated in 1954 to celebrate the undertaking's golden jubilee. It was also painted in the latest golden ochre and cream livery and may have been the first vehicle to carry this colour scheme. (*MDEKBC collection*)

Right and middle: The 1947 batch of Daimlers were quickly repainted into the livery carried by the 1949 Daimlers. These two shots show 75 (JKO 639) at the westbound Cannon stop and 76 (JKO 640) at the Mill Street stop on the Tovil service. Note that both buses have the crest that was discontinued in 1949. *(MDEKBC and W. J. Haynes/Author's collection)*

A later view of 81 (LKJ 781) passing County Hall on a Singlestone to Oxford Road working. It was displaying the smaller fleet name (without crest) and was an early repaint into the golden ochre and cream livery. *(W. J. Haynes via SEC)*

Carrying the same livery in this view is Brush-bodied Daimler 75 (JKO 639). It was pictured on a London Road working, just entering Maidstone Bridge. The line of traffic heading for the coast is a reminder of the congestion Maidstone experienced on summer weekends before the by-pass was opened. (*Author's collection*)

Beadle-bodied Crossley 36 (BKK 899) displays the immediate post-war version of the livery, which retained the extra brown band found on this pair of buses. It is standing at Mote Park on a cricket special, no doubt waiting for the end of play, in about 1947. (*John Parke/ Omnibus Society collection*)

All Crossley 43 (FKL 902) in the 1949 livery was photographed at Allington Way soon after the London Road service reached here on 6 March 1950, somewhat ahead of the housing development. Indeed, it was nearly twenty years before the orchard across the road was developed. (*MDEKBC/V. C. Jones*)

With the same Fremlins's advert on the front panel, 42 (FKL 901) was recorded standing at the Queen's Monument stop, although it is facing the wrong way to be heading to Tovil. (*MDEKBC*)

Definitely going to Tovil was 43 (FKL 902), photographed about 1953 in Mill Street in the then-current mainly dark brown scheme. Note that the Fremlins's advert had been updated and the apostrophe has been dropped from the name, which had several versions over the years. (*W. J. Haynes via SEC*)

No. 46 (GKK 985) was taken about 1955 in Sittingbourne Road on a working from Park Avenue to Tovil; it is in the golden ochre livery, but without the crest. (*Author's collection*)

Also in the same livery is 45 (GKK 984), again taken in Mill Street at the stop over the River Len, with Rootes's garage behind. (*MDEKBC*)

Guy Arab 52 (GKN 155) displays the initial post-war livery, complete with competing beer adverts, in this shot at the Queen's Monument while working the Penenden Heath to London Road service about 1949. (*MDEKBC*)

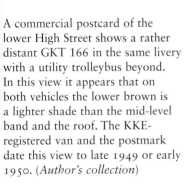

A commercial postcard of the lower High Street shows a rather distant GKT 166 in the same livery with a utility trolleybus beyond. In this view it appears that on both vehicles the lower brown is a lighter shade than the mid-level band and the roof. The KKE-registered van and the postmark date this view to late 1949 or early 1950. (*Author's collection*)

Photographed outside Granada House is Weymann-bodied Guy Arab 53 (GKN 156) in the 'more brown' version of the livery adopted in 1949. At this stage there was only one route and terminus in Shepway and hence the generic destination display used at this time. (*W. J. Haynes via SEC*)

When Week Street became one-way in 1927, outward Penenden Heath buses were routed via Pudding Lane. No. 59 (HKE 661), a Park Royal-bodied example, is picking up at the bus stop in Pudding Lane in this picture, which was taken in the early 1950s, in the dark brown livery, but with the large fleet name and no crest. (*MDEKBC*)

Above and below: The four Duple-bodied vehicles were easily identified by the thick pillar at the front upstairs. No. 48 (GKT 164) was captured by the photographer loading at the Queen's Monument – this view was taken after the extension of Shepway route to Oxford Road in 1952. Short workings to Derby Road necessitated the introduction of more specific destinations, as demonstrated by 50 (GKT 166), standing at the same stop a few years later in the company of a Crossley. (*MDEKBC/Author's collection*)

Many of Bill Haynes's pictures were taken in the afternoon and most were likely to have been taken on Saturday afternoon forays after work – as an office worker for London Transport in those days, he would have worked a five-and-a-half day week. A favoured location was outside Maidstone West station, no doubt on journeys to and from his home at Lewisham. An early afternoon view shows 51 (GKT 167) in dark brown. (*W. J. Haynes/Author's collection*)

An evening Bill Haynes view records the last Guy Arab, 61 (HKJ 480), in the golden ochre livery at the West Station. (*W. J. Haynes via SEC*)

No. 59 (HKE 661), also in golden ochre livery, was recorded at the junction of Knightrider Street and Mill Street. The building behind, formerly the Globe Inn, was demolished to ease the junction and to accommodate an extension to the Baptist church. (*Author's collection*)

Another view in Mill Street with 51 (GKT 167) heading for Tovil. This was the only Maidstone Corporation route to leave the town this way, although it was used by all the inward workings from the south of the town. (*W. J. Haynes via SEC*)

Above and below: Just the two HKE-registered Guy Arabs survived to carry the crest with the cream circle. No. 60 (HKE 662) was parked up between workings in the riverside car park in Fairmeadow around 1960. Also photographed here was a pair of Brush-bodied Daimlers, 79 and 81 (LKJ 779/81), displaying minor detail differences in their livery. Across the river, Maidstone's gas works can be seen. Until around 1970 the gas was produced by heating coal, which was delivered by barge. (*MDEKBC*)

In 1956, six Leyland Titans with Midland Red-style concealed radiators and Massey bodywork were delivered, enabling the last of the Crossleys to be withdrawn. Fleet numbers also reverted back to 1. Here, 2 (WKP 74) was photographed at London Road (Allington Way) in September 1956. (*Frank Wright/Richard Lewis collection*)

At the same location, Northern Coachbuilder-bodied Daimler 76 (JKO 640) was taken displaying the fleet name with the crest in a cream circle, dating this view to about 1960. Observe the building work in the background. (*Richard Lewis collection*)

A second batch of three Titans was received in 1957. No. 9 (999 AKT) had crossed a car coming down Tonbridge Road as it headed towards Rocky Hill, outside Maidstone West station. (*W. J. Haynes/Author's collection*)

Three more Titans arrived in 1958 and were the last to bear the crest without the cream circle. No. 10 (410 DKM) was recorded in Lower Stone Street passing the Granada cinema, soon after delivery, on a working to Oxford Road. (*Author's collection*)

1. From 21 June 1954, the Sutton Road route was extended to a new turning circle at Nottingham Avenue. This rare colour view of 54 (GKN 379) in the 'milk chocolate' brown and white livery was taken soon after the extension opened and shows the new housing in Nottingham Avenue, where the southern edge of Shepway reached the Sutton Road. (*Author's collection via Arnold Richardson*)

2. After the arrival of Walter Kershaw as General Manager in 1953, a number of livery experiments took place. At least three of the 1946 Sunbeams carried this application of ginger brown with two cream bands. No. 69 (HKR 8) was displaying this livery at Barming Bull Inn around 1955. (*Author's collection via Arnold Richardson*)

3. No. 63 (HKR 2) was captured as it turned at Barming Fountain Inn in 1965, using one of the two automatic frogs on the system. This was the basic version of the livery, with no lining out, but with the cream circle style crest. This was one of the trolleybuses withdrawn when the first Atlanteans arrived in 1965. (*Paul Hollingsbee*)

4. No. 71 (HKR 10) turns from Sutton Road into Wallis Avenue at the entrance to Park Wood estate. This was one of several sections of overhead to carry lights, to help drivers take the correct path in poor light. (*Paul Hollingsbee*)

5. *(Inset)* The final style of driver's cap badge. (*Author's collection*)

6. In 1960 the five wartime Sunbeams returned to service with new Roe bodies. No. 58 (GKP 513), with the blind already set for the return working, was recorded as it left the Fountain Inn for the Bull Inn. In the distance an Atlantean waits at the Fountain Inn terminus. (*Paul Hollingsbee*)

7. Ex-Brighton 51 (LCD 51) at Barming Bull Inn turning circle after its repaint in 1965 to the livery version with cream bands under the windows. (*Paul Hollingsbee*)

8. No. 64 (HKR 3) was recorded traversing Lower Stone Street – the background buildings were all demolished and replaced in the 1970s. (*Barry Ovenden*)

9. Northern Counties-bodied Daimler 79 (LKJ 779) in Pudding Lane during 1966 on a working on one of the infrequent routes that often terminated at the East Station. (*Ian Paterson*)

10. *(Inset)* Pre-decimal tickets. (*Author's collection*)

11. The last of the Titans, 26 (26 YKO), was recorded, along with the photographer's Morris Minor, near to the Westmorland Road terminus. (*Paul Hollingsbee*)

12. Kent Avenue was briefly used as the main terminus for the Shepway Estate and subsequently was used for peak hour short workings. No. 8 (998 AKT) was on layover here prior to working to Hackney Road. (*Paul Hollingsbee*)

13. The background at Oxford Road was remarkably similar, as the whole Shepway estate was very uniform, with 7 (997 AKT) in the foreground. (*Paul Hollingsbee*)

14. Reversing trolleybuses from the depot into the Tonbridge Road was always a difficult manoeuvre – in this view the conductor was looking for a gap in the traffic to bring 58 (GKP 513) into service. The tube that carried the bamboo pole can be seen under the rear panel. (*Barry Ovenden*)

15. Ex-Hastings 87 (BDY 810) was photographed in mid-reverse prior to taking up an evening peak working from Barming – a line of traffic had already built up, although the van in the foreground was parked. (*Barry Ovenden*)

16. Towards the end of trolleybus operations there were a number of enthusiast tours of the system. On Easter Sunday, 26 March 1967, the M&D and East Kent Bus Club hired ex-Brighton 52 (LCD 52). The group shot was taken at Park Wood. This vehicle had been fitted with an oval front grille following accident damage. (*Paul Hollingsbee*)

17. Sunbeam 72 (HKR 11) was decorated to commemorate the end of the trolleybuses. During the final week 72 toured the system a couple of times a day, but did not run in service. This view shows it in Upper Stone Street. (*Paul Hollingsbee*)

18. *Left:* On the final night, 72 conveyed the civic party from the town hall to depot. (*Paul Hollingsbee*)

19. *Above:* One of the 1946 Sunbeams being broken up at the premises of Matthews of East Malling, where many of the trolleybus fleet met their end. (*Paul Hollingsbee*)

20. Trolleybus replacement began in 1965 with the arrival of eight Massey-bodied Leyland Atlanteans, to an attractive design used only here and by Colchester Corporation (and a single example with A1 in Scotland) and introduced the light (Fiesta) blue and cream livery. No. 29 (EKP 229C) is seen when brand new at Barming Bull Inn. (*Paul Hollingsbee*)

21. A second batch of eight was delivered in early 1967 to complete the trolleybus replacement programme. At the Loose terminus, 40 (JKE 340E) was recorded soon after arrival and before the end of trolleybus operations. (*Paul Hollingsbee*)

22. To aid the trolleybus replacement, three Daimlers were retained much longer than the rest of the type. Brush-bodied Daimler 79 (LKJ 779) was photographed on 7 June 1968 joining Tonbridge Road from Queen's Road on a depot working on the Malling Terrace service. (*Mike Hodges*)

23. The third retained Daimler was a Northern Coachbuilders-bodied example, 75 (JKO 639), which was also treated to a repaint into the new livery. It was recorded at the Loose terminus on an evening peak extra in 1968. (*Ian Paterson*)

24. This view shows Leyland Titan 17 (517 RKR) departing from the Queen's Monument, also on the infrequent Malling Terrace service in 1968. It still looked smart despite being one of the last examples to retain the golden ochre livery. (*Ian Paterson*)

25. It was not until November 1968 that the final brown vehicles were withdrawn or repainted. On 6 June 1968 16 (516 RKR), one of the last brown Titans, was recorded passing Sharp's sports ground on an inward working from London Road. In the background is Buckland Lane, an earlier terminus of the London Road route. (*Mike Hodges*)

26. and 27. On Sunday 15 September 1968, much of Kent suffered torrential rain, which caused widespread flooding. By lunch-time on Monday the Medway had fallen enough to allow Corporation buses to ford the floods under the watchful eye of an inspector. Titans were mainly used (although I do have a not very good shot of one Atlantean going through the floods). No. 1 (WKP 71) heads for Allington Way, while in the opposite direction 20 (20 UKK) heads for Park Wood – the slip board shows it was on a rare working – one of two trips a day that were extended to serve Selby Road from 19 June 1968. Most of the buildings in the background have long gone – who remembers the Primrose & Len milk vending machines, as seen outside the Broadway Pie Shop? (*Paul Hollingsbee/Mike Hodges*)

28. From 1970, a new parking area in Museum Street was introduced for off-peak layovers. This view shows three Titans (7, 2 and 20) resting after the morning peak with a glimpse of the Maidstone Museum building behind. This area is now in the Fremlin Walk shopping complex. (*Ian Paterson*)

29. No. 4 (WKP 74) was working one of only four (five if it was a Saturday) East Station to Gatland Lane trips in 1972. It was recorded taking the corner from Week Street into St Faith's Street. Before April 1970 most buses would have continued straight down Week Street. (*Ian Paterson*)

30. The last two batches of Atlanteans delivered to Maidstone Corporation were bodied by Northern Counties, after they had bought out Massey's. First of the final batch, 51 (EKR 151L), was pictured as it was passing the Granada Cinema in about 1973 on the trunk route to Park Wood (*Author*)

31. Very few enthusiasts seem to have visited the Hackney Road terminus. Fortunately, Ian Paterson took this picture in 1972, just before all the workings were extended to Gatland Lane. Titan 12 (412 DKM) was recorded after it had reversed at the terminus and it stood awaiting departure. (*Ian Paterson*)

32. Utility Guy Arab HKJ 480 was retained after withdrawal and was converted to a recovery vehicle in 1960. It was initially painted green, but was repainted in yellow in 1970. This view shows it rescuing an Atlantean that had disgraced itself by failing in the High Street and causing traffic chaos. (*Author*)

33. No. 42 (JKE 342E) shows the simplified livery applied to a number of Atlanteans on repaint in 1972 and 1973. (*Author*)

34. (*Inset*) Post-decimalisation tickets. (*Author's collection*)

35. In 2004 a number of events took place to celebrate a hundred years since the introduction of the trams. At this time, former Maidstone Borough Operations Director Norman Kemp was in charge at Nu Venture and had two of this fleet painted into full Maidstone Corporation liveries. Former Dublin Olympian H838 FTW leaves Cornwallis School, Linton in February 2004 and represents the brown and cream livery.

36. In the final blue and cream colours, ex-London Leyland Titan A957 SUL works the last service 78 of the day, which continued in service to Nu Venture's depot at Aylesford, past the town hall in July 2004. How smart they both looked. (*Both Author*)

For the Diamond Jubilee of the undertaking in 1964, Titan 14 (414 GKT) was selected as the decorated motorbus. It was recorded in the lower High Street working a journey to Penenden Heath, with an ex-Hastings trolleybus behind. (*Author's collection*)

Just around the corner at the Pudding Lane stop, 23 (23 YKO) was photographed just after delivery in 1963. This was the first vehicle of the final batch of four Leyland Titans. The improved-style fibre-glass front end (known as a St Helens front after the first operator to use it) was fitted to the last three batches – totalling eleven vehicles – of Titans, which made them the PD2A model. Note the minor change to the livery application on this style of front. (*Author's collection*)

During the Corporation era, the Penenden Heath route ran via Sandling Road, Hope Street, Scott Street, Randall Street and Fisher Street to reach Boxley Road. In this view, 2 (WKP 74) was standing in Hope Street with 10 (410 DKM) behind. The year was 1963 and the reason for both buses being stopped and the general activity in the background was the fire, which destroyed St Paul's Church, blocking the route ahead. (*Richard Ratcliffe/MDEKBC*)

Titan 6 (WKP 76) had reached the terminus at Peel Street Hedges and was photographed basking in the sun, with the blind already set for its next working. (*MDEKBC*)

Two demonstrators were evaluated with a view to deciding on vehicles for the replacement of the trolleybus fleet. Wigan Corporation 49 (I IJP 4), Massey-bodied Leyland Titan PD3A, was tested in service during January 1964. It was just a longer, front-entrance version of the existing fleet, as can be seen from this view at Loose. (*MDEKBC*)

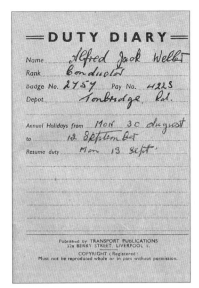

Above left: The other vehicle was a Leyland Atlantean demonstrator (SGD 669), with Alexander bodywork, which was later to become part of the Glasgow Corporation fleet. This was a more radical rear-engine design, although the model had been around since 1958 and Maidstone & District had an extensive fleet. It was recorded during its visit to Maidstone in May 1963 at Westmorland Road. (*MDEKBC*)

Above right: The 1965 duty diary of Conductor Weller recalls the time of the six-day week and rostered two weeks annual leave. For example one week, he worked his rest day, earning £22 6s 9d for a 58½-hour, seven-day week. (*Author's collection*)

The final view of this section gives a foretaste of things to come. Newly delivered Leyland Atlantean 32 (EKP 232C) is posed at the Barming, Fountain Inn terminus, with two Sunbeam trolleys on service behind. (*John Aldridge collection*)

Trolleybuses 1945–1967

Post-war, some of the English Electric trolleybuses survived long enough to be repainted in the new lighter livery. This official view shows a member of this batch in the new application. (*MDEKBC collection*)

A group of enthusiasts, the Southern Counties Touring Society, were regular hirers of Maidstone Corporation vehicles. On 28 March 1948 they hired 22 (KR 352) for a tour of the system. It was posed in the depot entrance, and in this view it looks rather dark as it was taken against the sun. A rear view taken at the same time also exists and the livery looks much lighter. Two versions of this view also exist – this one shows the bamboo pole hanging on its hooks on the body-side. (*Frank Wright via MDEKBC*)

It is thought that many of the utility vehicles gained a partial repaint into the new livery soon after the arrival of the new manager in 1946. This view of 54 (GKN 379) at the Queens Monument shows the band above the lower deck windows to be darker than the lower side panels. It is not, however, clear if the darker band is 'old' brown or black. (*W. J. Haynes via SEC*)

No. 57 (GKP 512), another utility in post-war condition, possibly with a lesser partial repaint; in this example the difference between the two shades is less obvious. (*W. J. Haynes via MDEKBC*)

From 22 May 1947, the trolleybus network was extended to Barming Bull Inn, just beyond the town boundary. Many journeys continued to terminate at the Fountain Inn and this view shows the overhead and three trolleybuses (in the first post-war livery) not long after the extension opened. (*Richard Rosa collection*)

Utility Sunbeam 64 (GKN 379) stands at the Bull Inn terminus about 1953, displaying the chocolate brown livery. (*Richard Lewis collection*)

No. 57 (GKP 512) displayed the post-1949 livery in this photograph at Barming Fountain Inn. The thick first pillar on the upper deck side windows is where the power cables travelled from the roof to the chassis. (*W. J. Haynes via SEC*)

Around the same time, sister vehicle 58 (GKP 513) was recorded setting down passengers on the Sutton Road opposite Mangravet Avenue. At this time, the service terminated at Grove Road. Observe the competing beer adverts carried by this vehicle. (*MDEKBC*)

No. 55 (GKN 380) is seen crossing Maidstone Bridge in the mid-1950s, unusually without a Fremlins's advert on the front, although alcohol still features. The town wharf building on Fairmeadow was demolished about 1960. (*Author's collection*)

Late in 1952, two Karriers with Roe utility bodies were purchased from South Wales Transport, where they had worked on the Llanelli system, which had just closed. They were stored for some time and it was not until January 1955 that the first example, 84 (CBX 533), entered service in the unique livery shown on the rear cover at Barming, Fountain Inn. By the time the second one entered service in August 1955 it carried the new colours, but had cream round the windows on both decks and was possibly the first trolleybus in this application. This picture shows 84 again at the West Station stop about 1958, when it had also been repainted in this latter style. (*MDEKBC*)

The second ex-Llanelli vehicle, 83 (CBX 532), was the last utility trolleybus to remain in service and was the only example to carry the crest on a cream circle. This shot was taken at the Tonbridge Road/Fant Lane junction. (*MDEKBC*)

All five of Maidstone's own utility trolleybuses were also repainted to carry this livery, as demonstrated by 54 (GKN 379). It was arriving at Loose when the terminal working was anti-clockwise – it was reversed in 1963. (*Lyndon Rowe via MDEKBC*)

Twelve Sunbeam trolleybuses were delivered during 1946/7, the largest single order ever placed by Maidstone Corporation, to replace the original fleet. First of the batch, 62 (HKR 1) displays the livery it carried from new at Barton Road. (*W. J. Haynes via SEC*)

Over their twenty-one years in service, they carried many liveries. The next livery was this less attractive, but more practical version with the white limited to the window surrounds. About 1949, 66 (HKR 5) was photographed at the Wheatsheaf junction, heading for Loose. The overhead for the Sutton Road route can be seen behind, while the point-work over the vehicle is the recently installed, but rarely used turning loop. (*W. J. Haynes/Author's collection*)

This view shows 67 (HKR 6) as it stood at the Grove Road terminus around 1950. It is in the same livery as the previous picture, but with the pre-1949 crest removed from the fleet name. (*W. J. Haynes via SEC*)

Back at the Wheatsheaf junction in around 1953, 71 (HKR 10) is now in the milk chocolate shade of brown with the small fleet name. Also visible is the divergence of the overhead between Sutton Road and Loose. This was one of two automatic frogs on the system – coasting took you to Sutton Road, while power on took the Loose route. (*W. J. Haynes/ Author's collection*)

No. 69 (HKR 8) was photographed in 1959 in Wallis Avenue on the Park Wood extension, in the standard golden ochre and cream livery. Note that once again the service had arrived while the housing was still being built. (*Author's collection*)

On a Grove Road short working, 69 (HKR 8) was photographed turning across the Sutton Road. The conductor is on the far side of the road, having pulled the release on the manual frog. (*Paul Hollingsbee*)

No. 66 (HKR 5) was decorated in both 1954 and 1964 for the golden and diamond jubilees of public service in Maidstone. This picture was taken in 1964 in Tonbridge Road. (*W. J. Haynes via SEC*)

In 1959 two Weymann-bodied BUTs came from Brighton Corporation. No. 51 (LCD 51) was sitting at Barming Fountain Inn, in its first livery application. (*MDEKBC*)

Later in 1959, the final second-hand purchase of trolleybuses was five Weymann-bodied Sunbeams from Maidstone & District's Hastings operation. Seen on its arrival at Maidstone is BDY 809 (later Maidstone 86), still behind M&D's AEC Regal towing vehicle, DKT 20. (*MDEKBC*)

In this view ex-Hastings 85 (BDY 807) was leaving the Nottingham Avenue turning circle to pick up an inward working of a short working to the High Street. (*MDEKBC*)

One reason for the short workings was to provide facilities to and from the Queen's Monument, which was only normally served by trips from Barming and towards Loose or Sutton Road. This is 88 (BDY 817) turning at the Queen's Monument to take up an evening peak working to Barming. (*MDEKBC*)

This picture shows ex-Hastings trolleybus 86 (BDY 809) on the Tonbridge Road near Hartnup Street. (*Barry Ovenden*)

After the opening of Bishop's Way, the main town centre stop towards Barming was this rather remote stop by the river. In this view, one of the ex-Brighton vehicles was standing by the very large shelter provided for passengers. Note how the overhead was pushed up by the booms and the second set of wires used by workings to the Queen's Monument. (*Author's collection*)

When this picture was taken, 57 (GKP 512) had just dropped some shoppers in Wallis Avenue, on the Park Wood loop. The new bodies on these vehicles were a foot longer, allowing six extra seats, and only had a life of seven years but the poorly built original bodies had reached the end of the road. (*Paul Hollingsbee*)

TROLLEYBUS SERVICES

MONDAY — FRIDAY   **LOOSE—PARK WOOD—BARMING**

	am	am	am		am	am	am		am	am		am	am	am
LOOSE........ dep.		6 00		6 20			6 34			6 50			7 00		
PARK WOOD..dep.	5 32		6 06			6 24		6 35			6 45			6 53	6 58 7 03
Nottingham Avenue..	5 35		6 09			6 27		6 37			6 47			6 57	7 02 7 07
Grove Road........	5 37		6 11			6 29	6*35	6 39			6 49	6 54	6 59		7 04 7 09
Wheatsheaf	5 40	6 05	6 14	6 25		6 32	6 38	6 39	6 42		6 52	6 55	6 57	7 02	7 05 7 07 7 12
Bishops Way........	5 46	6 13	6 20	6 33		6 40		6 47	6 50		7 00	7 03	7 05	7 10	7 11 7 15 7 20
West Station........	5 47	6 14	6 21	6 34		6 41		6 48	6 51		7 01	7 04	7 06	7 11	7 12 7 16 7 21
Milton Street........	5 51	6 18	6 25	6 38		6 45		6 52	6 55		7 05	7 08	7 10	7 15	7 16 7 20 7 25
Depot............	5 54	6 21	6 28	6 41		6 48		6 55	6 58		7 08	7 11	7 13	7 18	7 19 7 23 7 28
Barming, Fountain arr.	5 55	6 22	6 29	6 42		6 49		6 56	6 59		7 09	7 12	7 14	7 19	7 20 7 24 7 29
BARMING, Bull arr.	5 58						6 59				7 15				7 27

	am	am	am		am	am	am		am	am		am	am	am
LOOSE........ dep.	7 10				7 20		7 30			7 40			7 50		
PARK WOOD..dep.		7 08	7 13			7 18	7 23		7 28	7 33		7 38		7 43	7 48 7 53
Nottingham Avenue..		7 12	7 17			7 22	7 27		7 32	7 37		7 42		7 47	7 52 7 57
Grove Road........		7 14	7 19			7 24	7 29		7 34	7 39		7 44		7 49	7 54 7 59
Wheatsheaf	7 15	7 17	7 22		7 25	7 27	7 32	7 35	7 37	7 42	7 45	7 47	7 52	7 55 7 57 8 02
Bishops Way........	7 23	7 25	7 30		7 33	7 35	7 40	7 43	7 45	7 50	7 53	7 55	8 00	8 03 8 05 8 10
West Station........	7 24	7 26	7 31		7 34	7 36	7 41	7 44	7 46	7 51	7 54	7 56	8 01	8 04 8 06 8 11
Milton Street........	7 28	7 30	7 35		7 38	7 40	7 45	7 48	7 50	7 55	7 58	8 00	8 05	8 08 8 10 8 15
Depot............	7 31	7 33	7 38		7 41	7 43	7 48	7 51	7 53	7 58	8 01	8 03	8 08	8 11 8 13 8 18
Barming, Fountain arr.	7 32	7 34	7 39		7 42	7 44	7 49	7 52	7 54	7 59	8 02	8 04	8 09	8 12 8 14 8 19
BARMING, Bull arr.		7 37			7 47			7 57			8 07			8 17	

	am		am	am	am	am	am		am	am		am	am
LOOSE........ dep.	8 00		8 07		8 10			8 20			8 30		8 37
PARK WOOD..dep.		7 58		8 03		8 08	8 13		8 18	8 23		8 28	8 33
Nottingham Avenue..		8 02		8 07		8 12	8 17		8 22	8 27		8 32	8 37
Grove Road........		8 04		8 09		8 14	8 19		8 24	8 29		8 34	8 39
Wheatsheaf	8 05	8 07	8*12	8 12	8 15	8 17	8 22		8 25	8 27	8 32	8 35 8 37	8 42 8 42
Bishops Way........	8 13	8 15		8 20	8 23	8 25	8 30		8 33	8 35	8 40	8 43 8 45	8 47 8 50 8 50
West Station........	8 14	8 16		8 21	8 24	8 26	8 31		8 34	8 36	8 41	8 44 8 46	8 48 8 51 8 51
Milton Street........	8 18	8 20		8 25	8 28	8 30	8 35		8 38	8 40	8 45	8 48 8 50	8 52 8 55 8 55
Depot............	8 21	8 23		8 28	8 31	8 33	8 38		8 41	8 43	8 48	8 50 8 53	8 54 8 58 8 58
Barming, Fountain arr.	8 22	8 24		8 29	8 32	8 34	8 39		8 42	8 44	8 49	8 54	8 59
BARMING, Bull arr.		8 27			8 37			8 47			8 57		

*—To Queen's Monument.

A page from the 1966 trolleybus service timetable, showing some of the peak short workings. (*Author's collection*)

From 1959 to 1967, the former tram shed at Loose was rented for storage. The first use was to store utility trolleybuses prior to re-bodying. This September 1959 view shows 55 (GKN 380) with another by its side. The tram tracks were still visible in the foreground. (*Mick Comfort/Richard Lewis collection*)

In 1967 two withdrawn ex-Hastings trolleybuses, 86/7 (BDY 809/10), were stored here and raided for spare parts to keep the others running. (*Paul Hollingsbee*)

During wet or icy weather, it was necessary to change the carbon inserts in the booms during the day. This was achieved by sending out the tower wagon to the Barming Fountain terminus, which then parked in a less than traffic-friendly position to undertake this task. To facilitate this requirement the services interworked, so that all the vehicles in traffic got a layover at this point. (*Paul Hollingsbee*)

A de-wirement in traffic was never welcome. Here the driver of 65 (HKR 4) has taken the change of direction and gradient in the Broadway too fast and for his error has had to climb onto the roof to retrieve the booms – a health and safety nightmare! These have gone too high for the conductor's bamboo pole to reach. (*MDEKBC collection*)

Sunbeam 72 (HKR 11) was selected to be the official last trolleybus and was suitably decorated. It made its first appearance in this form on 9 April 1967 for a tour by the Southern Counties Touring Society. This view was taken at Loose during the tour and was one of at least three produced as postcards, no doubt to sell to members – notice only one person has a camera and how smartly they are dressed, with suits and ties. The picture also shows Inspector Jack Atkinson, who accompanied 72 right up until its final journey. (*Author's collection*)

On the last night, 54 (GKN 379) carried the senior staff and it was also partially decorated. (*MDEKBC collection*)

The official last trolleybus arrives at the depot just before midnight on 15 April 1967, with Inspector Jack Atkinson controlling the platform. (*Barry Ovenden*)

Maidstone Corporation Transport

Trolleybus Era 1928 - 1967

Ticket issued on
LAST TROLLEYBUS
Journey from TOWN HALL
MAIDSTONE to
JOURNEY'S END
11.30 p.m. 15th April 1967

Walter Kershaw M.Inst.T M.I.R.T.E
General Manager & Engineer

Special tickets were produced for the last journeys; they were yellow or blue depending which bus the passenger was travelling on. (*Author's collection*)

A sad view of a line-up of withdrawn trolleybuses stored at Maidstone Sack & Metal Co., Quarry Wood, Aylesford. (*Ian Paterson*)

The Blue Years 1965–1974

MAIDSTONE CORPORATION
TRANSPORT

TIME TABLE
AND
FARE TABLE

including all service alterations up to
27th JULY, 1970

Until Further Notice — Subject to Alteration

PRICE - - - - THREE-PENCE

This traditional style of timetable was used through the 1950s, right up until the penultimate issue in the 1970s. Each edition had a different coloured cover. (*Author's collection*)

Avove left and right: My first photos were taken on 4 April 1970, still on an Instamatic camera, the day before the major traffic scheme was introduced in the town centre. Leyland Atlantean 36 (JKE 336E), on the Westmorland Road service (a routing that lasted only 15 months), was followed by a Titan running empty back to depot heading south on College Road, while the second view shows Titan 26 (26 YKO) emerging from Week Street on the Allington Way service, the final day of both moves. (*Author*)

Another of my early pictures shows 23 (23 YKO) on an Oxford Road to Ringlestone working in Bishop's Way. In the background is the office of the former Maidstone & District Mill Street Bus Station. (*Author*)

Another change with the 1970 town centre traffic management scheme was to reverse the flow in Pudding Lane. This 1972 picture shows Titan 7 (997 AKT) emerging onto the High Street on a working from Ringlestone. (*Ian Paterson*)

Above and below: Routes begun in this period to serve new housing areas included those to Gatland Lane (from 4 June 1968) and Vinters Park (from 9 August 1971). I spent valuable pocket money to ride on these services and took these views of Titans 25 (25 YKO) at Gatland Lane and 20 (20 UKK) at the original Alkham Road/Birchington Close terminus in Vinters Park estate in 1971. (*Both Author*)

Above and below: Two shots taken about 1973 near my school; 10 (410 DKM) was heading for Oxford Road, past the former Mote Park Estate terminus, while 15 (415 GKT) was captured as it heeled round the bend on the edge of Mote Park. (*Both Author*)

Titan 12 (412 DKM) was recorded as it reversed at the Hackney Road terminus. This was an unusual arrangement in Maidstone, as most termini were provided with a turning circle. (*Ian Paterson*)

Brand-new Northern Counties Atlantean 47 (AKE 147K) at the Park Wood shops stand in 1971. Note that adverts were still being painted – a base white panel has been added to the between-deck panel. At this stage it was still conductor operated, as shown by the full rear destination display. When converted to driver only operation, the rear blind display was altered to show both ends of the route so it did not need to be changed on every trip. (*Ian Paterson*)

One of the final service developments during the Corporation era was the extension of occasional journeys on the Loose service beyond the former tram terminus to serve the village centre. These workings started from 12 March 1973 and 54 (EKR 154L) was recorded in a very rural part of the new route, displaying the rear blind style used for pay-as-you-enter services. (*Ian Paterson*)

The final Maidstone Corporation timetable, commencing 8 April 1973, was the only one to adopt a more modern image, complete with a photo of Atlantean 53 (EKR 153L) at Park Wood shops. It still did not include a route map!

MAIDSTONE CORPORATION TRANSPORT

TIME TABLE & FARE TABLE

INCLUDING ALL ALTERATIONS UP TO

8th APRIL, 1973

AND UNTIL FURTHER NOTICE

PRICE
3p

Young & Cooper Ltd., Maidstone

Epilogue

For many years these models, built by the depot staff, were on display. I remember them in the entrance hall to the Armstrong Road office, but this is a much earlier picture, taken in the Tonbridge Road office. (*John Aldridge collection*)

After 10 years stored at the depot, trolleybus 72 (HKR 11) went to Sandtoft Trolleybus Museum in 1977. In 1987 it was decorated for the twentieth anniversary of the end of trolleybuses in Maidstone. Behind is preserved 56 (GKP 511), which has been at Sandtoft since 1982. (*Author*)

The East Anglia Transport Museum at Carlton Colville, near Lowestoft, also has a working trolleybus facility and is home to former Brighton LCD 52, which retains its Maidstone Corporation livery – note also the original style grille has been restored. (*Author*)

To celebrate 100 years since the operation of the first trams, on 14 July 2004 a vehicle parade took place, running from the town centre to Barming and back. One of the buses in the parade was Arriva Dennis Dart 3176 (P176 LKL), which had been painted in Maidstone Corporation golden ochre and cream livery, albeit in Arriva style. (*Author*)

Although preserved trolleybus 72 (HKR 11) normally lives and operates at the Sandtoft museum in Lincolnshire, it is supported by the locally based 'Friends of 72'. From time to time it returns to Maidstone and it was towed around the parade route on 14 July 2004 and then displayed at the Queen's Monument. Technically it should be 'AFE 131A', as its original registration was transferred to a coach in 1984 and lost at the end of operations in 1992. (*Author*)

On Sunday 18 July 2004, a bus rally took place in Maidstone featuring a number of former Maidstone vehicles. Pride of place went to trolleybus 72 (HKR 11) and Leyland Titan 26 (26 YKO), which is now owned by local coach operator Alan Carr of Pluckley. (*Author*)

Fleet List

Trams

Fleet No.	Truck	Date Body
1–6	Brill 21E4	1904 Electric Railway & Tramway Carriage O26/22R
7	Brill 21E4	1905 Electric Railway & Tramway Carriage O26/22R
8–17	Brill 21E4	1907 United Electric O22/18R
18	Mountain & Gibson	1909 United Electric B19F
	Mountain & Gibson	1909 Water Car

Buses and Trolleybuses

Fleet No.	Reg. No.	Chassis	Date Body	Notes
1–3	KK 9418 – 20	Tilling-Stevens TS5	1924 Beadle B25F	
4–5	KL 1650 – 1	Tilling-Stevens TS6	1924 Beadle B36FR	
6–8	KM 3937 – 9	Tilling-Stevens LL	1926 Beadle B30C	
9–10	KP 319 – 20	Tilling-Stevens B10A	1928 Vickers B32R	
11	KO 8891	Ransomes D6 *	1928 Ransomes H32/31R	
12–13	KO 8543 – 4	Ransomes D6 *	1928 Ransomes H32/31R	
14–8	KO 8892 – 6	Ransomes D6 *	1928 Ransomes H32/31R	
19–22	KP 8371 – 4	Leyland Lion LT1	1929 Leyland B31R	
23–9	KR 351 – 7	English Electric *	1930 English Electric H30/26R	
30–1	KJ 6881 – 2	Tilling-Stevens C60A7	1932 Beadle B32R	
32–3	AKJ 49 – 50	Tilling-Stevens C60A7	1933 Beadle B32R	
34–5	AKO 390 – 1	Crossley Condor	1934 Crossley H24/24R	
36–7	BKK 899 – 900	Crossley Mancunian	1934 Beadle H24/24R	
38–9	CKO 70 – 1	Crossley Mancunian	1936 Park Royal H24/24R	
40–1	EKM 394 – 5	Crossley Mancunian	1937 Crossley H24/24R	
42–3	FKL 901 – 2	Crossley Mancunian	1938 Crossley H24/24R	
44–7	GKK 983 – 6	Crossley Mancunian	1940 Crossley H24/24R	
48–9	GKT 164 – 5	Guy Arab I 5LW	1942 Duple UH30/26R	
50–1	GKT 166 – 7	Guy Arab I 5LW	1943 Duple UH30/26R	
52–3	GKN 155 – 6	Guy Arab I 5LW	1943 WeymannU H30/26R	
54–5	GKN 379 – 80	Sunbeam W4 *	1943 Park Royal UH30/26R	RB
56–8	GKP 511 – 3	Sunbeam W4 *	1944 Park Royal UH30/26R	RB
59–60	HKE 661 – 2	Guy Arab II 6LW	1945 Park Royal UH30/26R	
61	HKJ 480	Guy Arab II 6LW	1945 Park Royal UH30/26R	
62–73	HKR 1 – 12	Sunbeam W4 *	1946 Northern Coachbuilders H30/26R	
74–6	JKO 638 – 40	Daimler CVG6	1947 Northern Coachbuilders H30/26R	
77–82	LKJ 777 – 82	Daimler CVG6	1948 Brush H30/26R	

83–4	CBX 532 – 3	Karrier W4 *	1945 Roe UH30/26R	XL
1–6	WKP 71 – 6	Leyland Titan PD2/20	1956 Massey H33/28R	
7–9	997 – 9 AKT	Leyland Titan PD2/30	1957 Massey H33/28R	
10–12	410 – 2 DKM	Leyland Titan PD2/30	1958 Massey H33/28R	
13–15	413 – 5 GKT	Leyland Titan PD2/30	1959 Massey H33/28R	
51–2	LCD 51 – 2	B.U.T. 9611T *	1951 Weymann H30/26R	XB
85–9	BDY 807/9/10/7/8	Sunbeam W4 *	1947 Weymann H30/26R	XH
16–18	516 – 8 RKR	Leyland Titan PD2A/30	1960 Massey H33/28R	
19–22	19 – 22 UKK	Leyland Titan PD2A/30	1962 Massey H33/28R	
23–6	23 – 6 YKO	Leyland Titan PD2A/30	1963 Massey H33/28R	
27–34	EKP 227 – 34C	Leyland Atlantean PDR1/1	1965 Massey H43/31F	
35–42	JKE 335 – 42E	Leyland Atlantean PDR1/1	1967 Massey H43/31F	
43	NKK 243F	Leyland Atlantean PDR1/1	1968 Massey H43/31F	
44	OKJ 844F	Leyland Atlantean PDR1/1	1968 Massey H43/31F	
45–6	OKM 145 – 6G	Leyland Atlantean PDR1/1	1968 Massey H43/31F	
47–50	AKE 147 – 50K	Leyland Atlantean PDR1A/1	1971 Northern Counties H43/31F	
51–4	EKR 151 – 4L	Leyland Atlantean AN68/1R	1972 Northern Counties H43/31F	

Notes: * – trolleybuses; RB – rebodied in 1960, Roe H34/28R; XL – ex-South Wales Transport 1952 (new to Llanelli), stored until 1955; XB – ex-Brighton Corporation, 1959; XH – ex-Maidstone & District (new to Hastings & District), 1959.

Withdrawal dates

About 1919: tram 18, water car; 1928–1930: trams 1–17; 1931: KK 9420; 1932: KK9418/9; 1933: KL 1650/1; 1934: KM 3937; 1936: KM 3938/9; 1940: KP 319/20, KP 8371–4; 1943: KJ6881/2, AKJ 49/50; 1945: AKO390/1; 1946: KO 8544/891/4, KR 351; 1947: KO 8543/892/3/5/6, KR 357; 1948: KR 352–6; 1949: BKK 899/900, CKO 70/1, EKM 394; 1955: EKM 395; 1956: FKL 901/2, GKK 983–6; 1957: GKT 166, GKN 155; 1958: GKT 165/7, GKN 156; 1959: GKT 164; 1960: HKJ 480 (%), CBX 532/3; 1961: JKO 638/40; 1962: HKE 661/2; 1963: LKJ 778/80–2; 1965: HKR 1/2/6/8/10/2, BDY 807; 1966: LCD 51, BDY 817; 1967: GKN 379/80, GKP 511–3, HKR 3–5/7/9/11 ($), LCD 52, BDY 809/10/8; 1968: JKO 639, LKJ 777/9; 1971: WKP 71–3/5; 1972: WKP 74/6, 997/9 AKT.

Remaining vehicles (18 Titans and 28 Atlanteans) transferred to Maidstone Borough Council, 1974.

Notes: % - converted to recovery lorry; $ retained by Maidstone Corporation as a preserved vehicle.

Body Codes used in fleet list: B – single-deck bus; H – Highbridge double-deck bus, followed by seating capacity, upper deck first; F – front entrance; C – centre entrance; R – rear entrance; U – utility body.

Livery Notes

Until 1965 the liveries were always based on brown (of different shades) and white or later cream in varying proportions. The period from 1935 to 1955 is particularly complex, partially due to wartime contingencies and then a rapid change of general managers in 1946, 1948 and 1953, with associated new policies. The exact details of this period were not fully recorded and there is some difficulty in trying to work out the livery from black and white photographs.

There were also several changes of fleet name and crest style over the years and these did not always coincide with livery changes.

The tram livery was brown (officially described as 'ochre') and off-white

The early bus livery was based on the tram livery, even to the extent of having an artificial division in the body-sides to mimic the rocker panel on the trams. On the trolleybuses the front and rears were brown, like the dashes of the trams. The first Crossley double-deckers (1934) introduced brown roofs and both batches of trolleybuses also had their roofs painted brown around this time.

From the late 1930s the shade of brown was lightened, except for a darker band over the lower deck windows. While many operators' utility buses were delivered in mainly grey or brown liveries, Maidstone Corporation's had virtually full pre-war livery, except for the grey roof and white wings. It was recorded that at least one utility trolleybus had a black band.

After the war, during Mr Johnston's brief tenure as manager, there was a major change to the livery. The 1946 Sunbeam trolleybuses and the 1947 Daimlers were delivered in a bright and simple livery of light brown beneath the lower deck windows and a band above.

Following a change of general manager, the 1949 Daimlers were delivered in a mainly brown scheme with just white around the upper and lower deck windows. Those loaned to London Transport were described as being a 'mustardy-brown'.

By 1953, the livery was a 'milk chocolate brown' applied to areas except for white on the lower deck window surrounds and at the same level on the staircase panel.

After the arrival of Mr Kershaw in 1954, an experimental livery was introduced with a lighter shade of ginger brown and cream, rather than white, relief.

The shade of brown was further changed to golden ochre and the first batch of Leyland Titans was delivered in 1956 in a standard version of this livery, with black lining-out. About this time the new coat-of-arms appeared, and from 1958 the crest was placed on a cream circle to improve the contrast against the brown. Some older vehicles did not have the lining-out and some gained more cream on their second repaint in this livery.

Delivery of the first Leyland Atlanteans in late 1965 introduced Fiesta blue in place of the golden ochre livery. Black lining-out was continued between the colours, but the roof and domes were cream. This livery was used for all the Atlanteans and all twenty-six Titans and one Daimler (75 – JKO 639) were repainted into this livery, so that the golden ochre livery was eliminated by November 1968.

Towards the end of the Corporation period, some minor detail changes were made to simplify the livery on the Atlanteans.

Select Bibliography

The Tramways of Kent (Volume 1) by 'Invicta' (Light Railway Transport League, 1972)

The Maidstone Trolleybus 1928–1967 by D. J. S. Scotney (National Trolleybus Association, 1972)

75 Years of Municipal Transport in Maidstone by Richard Lewis and Eric Baldock (M&D and East Kent Bus Club, 1979)

Maidstone and Chatham Tramways by Robert J. Harley (Middleton Press, 1994)

Maidstone Trolleybuses by Robert J. Harley (Middleton Press, 1997)

Maidstone Corporation Illustrated Fleet History (M&D and East Kent Bus Club, 2004)

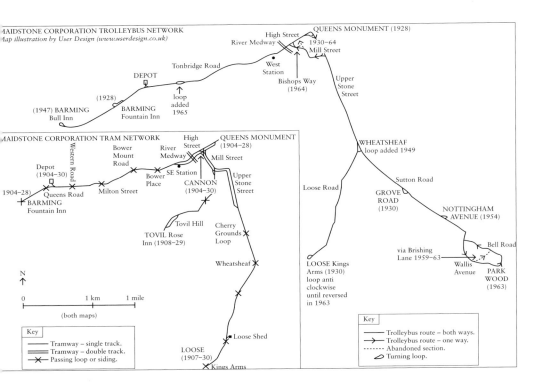

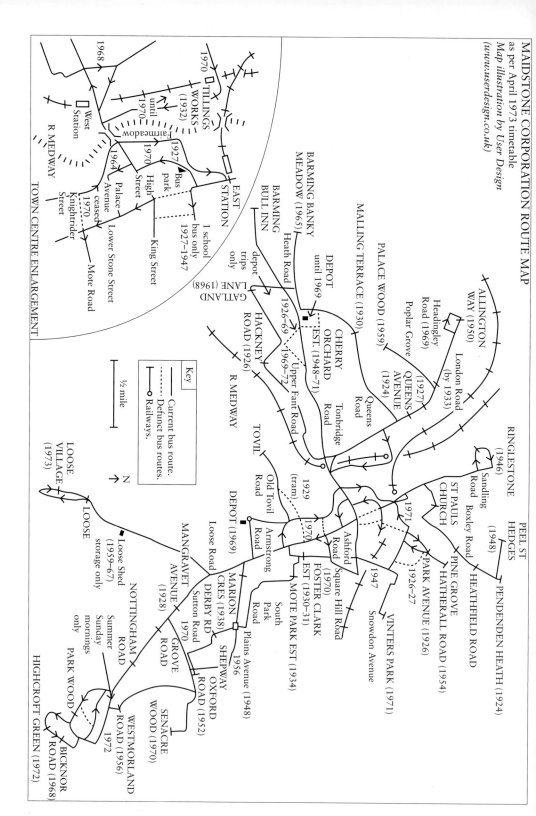

MAIDSTONE CORPORATION ROUTE MAP
as per April 1973 timetable
Map illustration by User Design
(www.userdesign.co.uk)

TOWN CENTRE ENLARGEMENT

96